T0194199

Turning the World Right Side Up

Claiming the Earth for Christ

ROBERT A. JONES

iUniverse, Inc.
Bloomington

iUniverse books may be ordered through booksellers or by contacting:

iUniverse
1663 Liberty Drive
Bloomington, IN 47403
www.iuniverse.com
1-800-Authors (1-800-288-4677)

ISBN: 978-1-4502-7967-3 (sc)
ISBN: 978-1-4502-7968-0 (ebook)

Printed in the United States of America

iUniverse rev. date: 01/18/2011

To Jesus Christ

Who was and is
God the Son
Emmanuel
The Lamb of God
The Savior of the World
The Risen Lord
The Great "I Am"
The Good Shepherd
The Door of the Sheep
The Living Word
The Light of the World
The Way, the Truth, and the Life
The Living Vine
The Faithful Friend
The Divine Bridegroom
The Prince of Peace
The Alpha and the Omega

Preface

Back in 1964, the Spirit wrote indelibly on my mind the words of a speaker: "The renewal of the church in the future will take the shape of recovering the New Testament form of faith and experience." During that same year, I encountered Christ as the Bible came alive and I saw Jesus as the unique God/man. Those experiences defined my Christian journey for the rest of my life. From that time forward, I went to the New Testament committed to reshape my faith and experience by what the apostles taught who were as close to Jesus (God/man) as we will ever get. I would discover the difference between Christianity when it began and as we find it twenty centuries later

Mathematics was my major in college leading to a B.S. and M.S. After entering the ministry and encountering the Lord, I went on to graduate school in Biblical studies to pursue a Ph.D. as I was planning to do in mathematics. After two years, it became clear I would not learn there the practical wisdom the apostles taught those first Christians on how to walk with Christ in their daily lives. I saw that we learn New Testament truth not by simply reading and studying but making the journey of discipleship and servanthood. The Spirit led me to return to the pastorate and shape my own life and ministry to others by what I was learning about New Testament Christianity.

Those two years did equip me with primary sources for study as well as helping me to go to the Bible in the original languages when that would help to clarify the original meaning.

One invaluable study during these years consisted of examining key Greek words related to the faith and experience of the first Christians, that translate into such words as gospel, truth, new, creation, faith, justification, righteousness, sanctification, holiness, salvation, birth, perfection, appearing, coming, revelation, kingdom, calling, election, authority, power, freedom, etc. Such words may be foreign to many Christians today, but they were an integral part of the faith and experience of the first Christians. When understood, they help us appropriate God's grace and grow in our faith as we learn to walk with Christ. By listing Paul's letters in chronological order, and studying the words as they appear in his letters, one can then trace the spiritual progress of the first Christians as the Spirit led Paul and them from spiritual infancy to maturity. One can also observe some new words that emerge in the later epistles as well as the fulfillment of earlier expectations related to Jesus' Return!

This book is a result of my spiritual journey, pastoral ministry, scriptural study, and journaling, the latter to help me remember the lessons the Lord was teaching me along the journey. I believe it accurately presents the faith and experience of the apostles. Their focus was on *Jesus, His word, and His kingdom.* This is the banner this book seeks to raise for the church today that it may awaken to its role of leading the way to claim the earth for Christ.

Contents

Introduction

Very early in my quest to read the New Testament afresh, I discovered that Jesus and the writers of the New Testament believed He would return for His first followers. In fact, as I discovered more verses, I came to believe this in a few months and historical research along with ongoing Biblical study in the following years confirmed it. The appendices in this book present Biblical and historical information so readers may see the basis for this.

The first sixteen chapters present New Testament Christianity looking at its roots in the Old Covenant, its beginnings, and then the process of spiritual growth through the New Covenant. Where New Testament Christianity differs from present day Christianity is in the following chapters. Jesus and the apostles taught He would return back then.

Chapters 17–21 tell about the climax to Christian faith and experience expected when Jesus returned. We will look at the signs Jesus gave to His disciples so they would know when that event was about to happen. Paul taught about Jesus' Return during their lifetime from the very beginning of his ministry. The Revelation and the latter letters witness that the time had come for Jesus' Return. Those same letters also report that earlier expectations related to Jesus' Return began to occur in the lives of those first Christians.

Chapters 22–27 deal with what it means to live in a world where Jesus returned. Paul said the ends of the ages had come upon his generation. We shall look at the biblical ages that concluded during the apostolic generation and what it means for us to live in the period between Jesus' Return and history's grand finale of peace on earth. We shall look at God's strategy to accomplish this great vision.

The roots of the Protestant Church go back to the Reformation that established Scripture as our highest authority. That helped the church clarify the beginning and growth of Christian faith and experience, but it never dealt, for the most part, with the climax related to Jesus' Return. I believe God is leading the church to finally do that today, to examine church doctrine more carefully by the light of Scripture.

A lot is at stake. If Jesus returned back then, peace is possible on earth and the missing piece to realize the dream is not waiting for some future action by God, but a "now" response by Christians to learn and live God's way as taught in the New Testament.

The Thessalonians were saying that those New Testament Christians were turning their world upside down. God would have said it differently. Because of sin, their world already had been turned upside down from what God planned when He made us in His own image. God in His grace acted through Jesus and made a New Covenant providing everything we needed to get our lives and relationships together. Now God needs New Testament Christians like those at Thessalonica who, as God would put it, *turn their part of the world right side up.*

1

The Sleeping Giant

During Christmas, 1975, God gave me a special dream where I was the quarterback on this football team. Huge defensive linemen were waiting to destroy me. I had one offensive lineman, the center, whom I came to call the "Magnificent Lineman." He also called the plays. As long as I huddled with him, got *his* play, and followed *his* interference, I could not be stopped. I went in for touchdown after touchdown. Then I decided to call a play on my own, an end-run. There was only one problem. The "Magnificent Lineman" did not run interference this time and I was smeared. The lesson was clear. Learn to huddle with the Lord, get God's plays, and then combine faith in God's power to lead and clear the way along with obedience and following God's plan.

God was showing me New Testament Christianity. The Twelve had learned to huddle with Jesus (God in the flesh), walking with Him for three years. He taught and demonstrated lessons from God's playbook. After His Resurrection, they spent fifty days huddling in prayer before pursuing God's plan. Then they followed the Lord as He led them to spread the gospel in a hostile world. Despite persecution that resulted in much martyrdom, they could not be stopped as they reached throughout the known world of their day.

The church today for the most part does not display such power. Too many "end-runs" since the apostolic generation have been worked into God's playbook resulting in activity where God's power is not a factor. I believe God is leading His people today back to Jesus, His word, and His kingdom. There we will discover the faith and experience of the apostles and the wisdom that enabled them to take the gospel to their world despite intense opposition.

Paul exhorts the Ephesians: "Wake up, O sleeper" (5:14 NIV). He tells about amazing things in this late letter that are happening for Christians during those days when, I believe, Jesus was returning and appearing to the faithful. We will look at these later on in this book. Paul is praying that God will give them revelation and wisdom (1:17) to understand these things that open new and exciting discoveries and possibilities for their faith while still on this earth.

The giant referred to in the title of this chapter is the church. This is not because Christians are better than others, but because we are uniquely linked to the living God through Jesus and the indwelling Holy Spirit. We have the written record of God's playbook and access to His kingdom power. I believe God is bringing the church back to the faith and experience of the apostles, to take time to huddle with Jesus, to get God's plays, to follow His leading, and to trust in His power to clear the way. Then the church will not be stopped in reaching the world for Christ and leading the way to God's grand finale of peace on the earth.

2

Waiting, Waiting, and Still Waiting

United Methodist Bishop Wayne Clymer, back in the sixties before assuming that position, began his address to a national gathering of E.U.B. men in a fictitious dialogue with Niketa Kruschev who was experienced in revolutions. Prior to Clymer's meeting with Christian revolutionists, he asks the Russian premier for any counsel he might give.

Khrushchev asks about the strengths and resources. Clymer says there are 64 million members, 381 thousand leaders with 4–7 years of training, and 290 thousand centers of instruction. They spent 984 million dollars on new construction (1961 figures). Impressed by such resources, Khrushchev asks how they are situated in society. Clymer reports that we have cells in every village and meeting places in every community. Our handbook on revolution (Bible) is in nearly every home. We have infiltrated every section of society. Khrushchev replies. "What are you waiting for? Take over."

I will tell you what the church was waiting for then and is waiting for now: the Second Coming of Jesus when He begins to reign along with a variety of ideas about what that means. (It is much easier to understand the Second Coming when you can look back after the fact rather than speculate about what the prophecies mean.) The formation of Israel in 1948, the end of that generation in 1988, the start of a new millennium in 2000 excited some people during my lifetime to believe Jesus' Return was near. Events in the Middle East lead some Christians to still look for His Return soon, and we still wait. In fact, we have been waiting for nearly 2,000 years. Jesus and His apostles said He would return back then. Their witness is reported in the New Testament that became Scripture. It is time for the church to go back to the New Testament and let Scripture, not past tradition, determine our thinking about the time of the Second Coming.

The attitude of many Christians today toward the Return of Jesus can be described by apathy or eagerly seeking prophetic signs pointing to Jesus' Return. Neither describes how the apostles prepared the first Christians. Anything but apathetic, they were taught Jesus' Return was that awesome moment when they would give an accounting of their lives and the faithful would be rewarded. The apostolic preparation focused not on prophetic signs, but learning the kingdom way God wanted us to live. Paul's later epistles reveal the discoveries made by the faithful during their last days. God waits for us today to recover the faith and experience of the apostles from the beginning to its climax as revealed in Scripture. This is the kingdom cooperation God needs to take over this earth, not by force, but Spirit-empowered obedient and witnessing servants going on to maturity.

3

The Prophetic Vision

God gave to the world through the Hebrew prophets a vision of a future day when the peoples of this earth would live together in peace. God sent His Son Jesus to show by example and teaching how we need to live in order to do our part to bring it about. God made through Jesus a New Covenant whereby each repentant and believing person is forgiven and receives the Holy Spirit. That indwelling Spirit makes us God's children and links us with the resources necessary to change us into people like Christ who will be makers of the peace, *if we are willing to do things God's way.*

Peace is impossible for the race of the first Adam. We all fell to sin, misused our free will, disregarded God's will, pleased our own desires, and pursued the lies of Satan and his hosts with their aim to destroy lives and relationships. God in His love and wisdom revealed through Jesus His plan to redeem us and create a new humanity, fashioned after the person of Jesus Christ whom the apostle Paul referred to as the last Adam.

Those who share the life of Jesus, the last Adam, and follow His example are the kind of people who will be able to live together in peace. They repent of sin and turn from the life of the first Adam that filled this earth with selfishness, greed, lies, hatred, violence, murder, fornication, adultery, homosexuality, etc. They become disciples of Jesus by learning His instruction, obeying His commands, following His example as a servant, and relying on His mercy when they stumble into sin.

No human being or organization, such as the United Nations, will ever bring peace to this earth. The race of the first Adam will never pull it off. Only God can accomplish this and as we shall see in this book, He has already done His part. He provided victory over sin, death, and the powers of evil before which we were powerless. Now we must appropriate what the apostles experienced and work with the One who now is orchestrating peace on this earth.

I remember Fred Craddock telling the story about a mother trying to entertain a child at home. She cut up a picture of a map of the world that was in the newspaper and challenged him to put it together. Much to her surprise, he accomplished this in a short period of time. She asked how he did it so quickly. He said on the other side of the map of the world was the picture of a man, and *if you get the man right, you put the world together.* God sent Jesus into the world to show us how to get it right, and then made a New Covenant to make it possible for us to follow in His footsteps and also get it right. Let us see what we can learn from Jesus, the Prince of Peace.

4

The Kingdom Revolution

I have seen during my lifetime three major revolutions seeking worldwide domination. Adolph Hitler and his book *Mein Kampf* inspired the first. Next came the communist cause based on *The Communist Manifesto* by Karl Marx. Now we are seeing the Islamic terrorist revolution inspired by its interpretation of *The Koran* written by Mohammed. All of these revolutions advanced their causes by using violence and war to impose their ways upon others.

In contrast, Jesus introduced the kingdom revolution of servanthood advanced not by force but by gaining the freewill response of people. The Sermon on the Mount in Matthew 5–7 summarizes His teaching. While Holy War occurred under the Old Covenant, Jesus made it clear a new day had dawned in the providence of God as He taught His followers to love and pray for their enemies leaving vengeance into God's hands. Jesus taught His followers to pray for the coming of this kingdom and to seek it first along with its righteousness in their daily lives. He demonstrated the kingdom's power to heal the sick, raise the dead, and cast out demons.

The kingdom of God referred to what life would be like on this earth *when we do things God's way,* in other words, submit to His rule and reign over our lives. Jesus pioneered this new "straight and narrow way" of living in obedience to the heavenly

Father. Facing that terrible death for our sin, He asked the Father if that cup could be taken from Him concluding His prayer with "not my will, but yours be done." Diametrically opposed to the course we took on this earth through sin and disobedience and still take, Jesus obeyed His Father's commands and taught His disciples this kingdom way. He commanded them to perpetuate this process by making disciples of all nations, teaching them to observe the same commands so this unique way Jesus lived and taught would spread. Jesus started this kingdom revolution: obey God and seek His will, part of His overall plan to someday bring peace to our earth. *What Would Jesus Do?* His apostles knew and lived that way back then. Faithful disciples are learning from them and doing that today.

It is difficult for us who live in a democracy to understand the nature of a kingdom. We elect our leaders and decide the laws that will govern our society. God doesn't leave those decisions up to us in His Kingdom. He has chosen Jesus to be king and tells us in His word the righteousness by which the King governs. Would you like to take part in a revolution that will someday bring peace to this earth? Then embrace Jesus' kingdom way that you will learn in the New Testament from those who learned from Jesus.

5

The King

Who is Jesus anyway? Why is anybody who lived on earth deserving of such devotion? The New Testament says He was more than just a man. Jesus was God in human form. He is the only person on earth who made the claim to be Divine stand the test of time. Millions through the centuries to this day have thus worshiped Him as His first followers came to do.

His first disciples came to believe He was the promised Messiah. At His birth, an angel announced Jesus was the descendant of David to whom God's kingdom would be given (Luke 1:32-33). Peter said Jesus was the prophet foretold by Moses to whom his race must listen or be cut off from God's people (Acts 3:22–23). Paul said Jesus was the descendant of Abraham who would give the Holy Spirit, the blessing of Abraham, to the world (Gal. 3:14).

God's kingdom was present for a while on earth tied to the nation of Israel. Prophets, priests, and kings were needed. All of these offices were necessary for God in His holiness to dwell in the midst of a sinful people. This arrangement under the Old Covenant never worked as these leaders along with the people seldom kept covenant and obeyed God. Jesus fulfilled these roles in Himself through the New Covenant. Jesus was the prophet who was and spoke the word God wanted us to hear. He atoned for the sins of all people by serving as both sacrificial Lamb and high priest. Jesus was the descendant of David and the Father's choice to receive the kingdom that operated on earth under King David during the days of the Old Covenant.

God's king would reign in love. He would exercise the authority and power of God but with compassion and mercy. During His days on earth, He did not live as the Lord of heaven He really was, or as the King of the earth that He would become. He rather took the form of a servant. He called people to follow Him in this way of servanthood as His disciples, but He never forced them. He laid it on the line regarding the great divide that separated us on earth from His Father. He offered God's grace enabling us to cross the divide and become His children and possess a great hope of someday living forever in His heaven. The choice would be up to each of us.

At His Return, Jesus would take authority over the earth from Satan. He would also receive the kingdom limited to Israel under the Old Covenant, but opened to anyone from any nation under the New Covenant. Churches were filled after 9/11 for at least a few weeks. How bad it must get before we finally agree to do it God's way remains to be seen. The climax is not in doubt, only how long it will take to get us to *work with the reigning King on His terms.*

6

The New Covenant

The Old Covenant never worked. The prophets tell of God's many warnings unheeded by the people. Judgment came upon them in 587 B.C. as the Babylonians destroyed the temple and removed the Jewish people from their land for seventy years. God promised to bring them back and told about a New Covenant He would make with them in the future. This would be of such a superior nature that it would go out to all peoples of the earth.

Jeremiah 31:31–34 speaks about this New Covenant where God will put His laws in the minds of His people and write them upon their hearts so they will finally obey. Ezekiel 36:25–27 says God will accomplish this by putting His Spirit in them. The Holy Spirit provided a new dimension through the New Covenant working in the hearts of faithful disciples to help them turn from sin and the old nature to the righteousness and love of God revealed in Jesus. We were made in His image and likeness and now God had put in place what was needed to redeem what had been lost through sin.

Jesus made this possible through His death on the Cross-where He endured our punishment and offered Himself as a sacrifice to atone for our sin. This satisfied God's justice and freed us from condemnation and guilt under the law. Through this New Covenant mercy and grace where God ended the law's sin-reckoning process under the Old Covenant, we are not only forgiven our sin but also accounted as righteous. He gives us the Holy Spirit whereby we become His children and part of His family on earth, the Body of Christ. He disciplines us as a Father who loves His children when we sin or go astray. The Holy Spirit will also convict us of our sin at such times and provide needed counsel to help us get back on the kingdom track.

This New Covenant went first to the Jewish people and then to the Gentiles. The Old Covenant limited to the people of Israel was not an eternal covenant and ended in A.D. 70 with the destruction of the temple and the ending of animal sacrifices to atone for sin. This New Covenant will last forever. God has provided through it all we need to turn our lives around and follow in the way Jesus pioneered before us. The Holy Spirit will form in the faithful who keep covenant by trusting God's grace and following in Jesus' kingdom way the same life that was in Jesus. The Spirit will transform us into the kind of persons who will occupy heaven and someday bring peace to the earth.

The New Covenant is sufficient to accomplish all this. God now needs disciples who will submit to the authority of Jesus' Father and follow in the kingdom revolution led by Jesus that we learn in the New Testament. Everything is in place. Now, we just need to *read the directions, obey, and work with the reigning King to turn our part of the world right side up.*

7

The Authoritative Writings

The second member of the Godhead lived on this earth for a brief period of time in the person of Jesus, the Jewish Messiah. He called twelve men to be with Him for about three years. Prophets and righteous men from the past longed to see those days when the Lord of heaven would live on earth. The Twelve had that opportunity to see and hear the Word made flesh.

After His Crucifixion, Resurrection, and initiation of a New Covenant, Jesus sent the Third Member of the Godhead to help the apostles remember and understand what Jesus had taught. The Holy Spirit would expand their understanding as the disciples matured and took the gospel into the world.

Jesus is the only person who ever lived on earth whose teaching was infallible. Unfortunately, He never left any writings. The closest we will ever come to truth, knowing God, and understanding the way He wants us to live will be found in the writings of the primary apostles. They were with Jesus during His time on this earth and then taught by the Holy Spirit who immediately followed. He brought them through the sanctification process to maturity and inspired the witness they left for us in the New Testament.

By primary apostles I mean The Twelve personally chosen and mentored by Jesus during those three years, and then to whom (minus Judas) the Risen Jesus appeared after His Resurrection.

Paul would replace the betrayer Judas and was personally called by the Risen Jesus. Paul was not privileged to know Jesus when He lived on earth, but was taken up into the Third Heaven where he was prepared for his special mission to take the gospel into the Gentile world. By way of contrast, men voted secondary apostles into office. Matthias is such an example in the Book of Acts followed by the Popes or Bishops of Rome identified by the Roman Catholic Church as apostles succeeding Peter. Secondary apostles chosen by men never had the direct experience with Jesus, as did the primary apostles.

No generation will ever surpass what those primary apostles learned and experienced during their generation, as we will see in this book. They learned from the living God and witness about these discoveries in the New Testament. It tells of a spiritual journey beginning with converts turning from sin, trusting in God's grace, receiving the Holy Spirit, obeying Jesus' commands, and serving with the spiritual gifts He gave them. This journey climaxed in producing mature, Christlike persons. Can the church ever do any better than this? I don't think so. That is why we have to go back to the authoritative writings in order to learn and do it God's way.

8
The Betrothal

Paul told converts that they now were betrothed to Christ. He wanted them to understand that they had begun a personal journey with the living God through Jesus. That very image of the betrothal between a man and a woman on this earth helped beginning believers to understand that it is an intimate relationship that Jesus wants with His people.

Jesus taught similarly while on earth. In fact, John the Baptist, the forerunner of the Messiah, referred to Jesus as the Bridegroom coming for His people. According to John in his Gospel, Jesus performed His first miracle at a marriage feast, a sign pointing to how God was saving the best for last after the failure of the Old Covenant. When asked why His disciples did not fast like the followers of John the Baptist, Jesus said they did not fast because the Bridegroom was with them. In the future, Jesus would be taken from them and then they would fast, as the Holy Spirit would prepare them to be joined in spiritual union with Jesus when He would return. At that time, He would take the faithful as His bride to live forever with Him and the Father in heaven.

This is amazing! Jesus wants to develop a love relationship with you and me. Let me reflect upon who Jesus is for us. He came from His Father to be the Lamb of God who would take away our sin. He gave those who responded to the gospel the living water of the Holy Spirit to begin in them the same life shared by Jesus and

His Father. He provided living bread and drink to nurture this eternal life begun by the living water of the Holy Spirit that He later identified as the bread (His body) and the wine (His blood) at the Last Supper. Here we remember His atoning death. He was the light of the world to show the way leading to heaven. He was the truth that would set people free. He was the true vine offering an intimate relationship with Himself like branches connected to their vine. He was the Resurrection promising eternal life for all who would trust Him. He was the Lion of the tribe of Judah who would provide for victory over sin, evil, and death. He was David's descendant who would reign over God's kingdom in this world. All things were created through Him at the beginning and history will climax in peace under His reign. We learn this in the authoritative writings.

Wow! We are betrothed to this One now who wants someday to be joined to us as His bride. That is mind-boggling and powerfully motivating to turn from all sin, serve Jesus, love others, and cooperate with the work of the Holy Spirit. He transforms us to be like Christ so we may take our place someday with Him in the heaven He has prepared for those who love Him.

9

The Way

The prophet Isaiah told about a spiritual highway that would emerge in this sin-cursed world. "It shall be called the Highway of Holiness" (Isa. 35:8). It would lead people to heaven and into the Presence of God that had been lost because of sin. Following Babylon's removal of the Jews from their land in 587 B.C. because of breaking covenant with God, Isaiah 40 speaks comfort and tells of a future voice of hope crying in the wilderness that would be fulfilled by John the Baptist. "Prepare the way of the Lord; make straight in the desert a highway for our God" (Isa. 40:3). John called people to repent and follow Jesus up this Highway of Holiness to heaven.

Jesus taught this kingdom way and said that He Himself was the Way leading to the Father. Right in this world of sin, corruption, evil spirits, and death, Jesus walked the straight and narrow way of the kingdom of light. He left behind wherever He went a trail of truth, righteousness, holiness, love, and good deeds. He left in the minds of His disciples a vivid picture of how God wanted us to live. Committed to doing the Father's will and taking the form of a servant, Jesus said this way leads to His Father from whom Jesus came to save us. Unlike the broad way of sin and selfishness that leads to broken lives, broken relationships, and death, Jesus showed us the higher way God intended for us from the beginning when He made us in His own image and likeness.

The kingdom way was not easy for Jesus or His followers. Jesus was crucified and told His followers they must learn to deny themselves, take up their crosses, and follow after Him. In another place, He said to count the cost to see if they were up to it, quite a contrast to the way in which the Christian life is often presented today. The mission of the early church was to make disciples who by definition learn and obey the commands of Jesus. He expected an all-out commitment from His followers to walk the kingdom way of holiness, righteousness, and servanthood.

God preserved this kingdom way of living by revealing its truths in the twenty-seven New Testament books of life. The Gospels tell about the life of Jesus. Acts tells about the ministry of Peter and Paul as they spread the Good News of this new life among the Jews and Gentiles. The Epistles tell how new converts were changed through the Holy Spirit by following the apostles' teaching. Disciples in all generations making the same journey will be able to understand what they need to know as they read these books of life. The Holy Spirit will teach them directly and utilize spiritually gifted teachers to shed light on this Highway of Holiness.

10
Roadblock #1 – Unbelief

Unbelief about Jesus Christ is the great roadblock on the kingdom Highway of Holiness that someday will lead to peace. He is the only hope. I can make this claim because only the New Covenant provides for the forgiveness of sins and the gift of the Holy Spirit that can transform sinful persons into servants like Christ. The same love that shone through Jesus Christ in His ministry is the same love the Holy Spirit works in the hearts of faithful disciples. Such persons on the road to become like Christ are the kind of people who will lead the way to peace on earth.

Many people back then had a hard time believing in the Divinity of Jesus. He once replied to a person asking for a miracle yet doubting Jesus could do it: "If you can believe, all things are possible to him who believes" (Mark 9:23). Jesus' disciples also had a hard time believing He was God. His words "O ye of little faith" expressed His frustration time and again at their slowness to believe who He was and that with God all things are possible.

Paul found this same difficulty to believing in the God/man Jesus when taking the gospel to the intellectual center of Greek culture in Athens. There is no record of Paul making any converts there. They listened until Paul talked about the resurrection from the dead. That was more than their intellectually limited minds could handle. The virgin birth, the many miracles, and His Resurrection from the dead all defy the limits of human reason, making faith for many difficult. Unfortunately, with the passage of time, Jesus has been reduced in many parts of the church to little more than a human being and a great teacher like other religious leaders.

I heard of a man who left Christianity because he was glad to find a religion where he did not have to park his brains at the door. Rather than park our brains at the door, it is much better to park our unbelief. Then, faith rooted in God's word enables us to trust what Jesus did at the Cross, so we may know with assurance that we are forgiven and reconciled to God. Such faith in God's word enables us to appropriate the reality of the Holy Spirit in our hearts. Then we can utilize our minds to understand truth as the Holy Spirit gives us light. Our faith grows as we study Scripture and make the disciple journey.

"Therefore whoever hears these sayings of Mine and does them…" (Matt. 7:24). It is not enough just to study what Jesus taught. We are to do the word. New Testament faith is a living faith meaning it acts. As we huddle with the Lord in prayer, embracing His promises and see answers, pursuing His leadings and see results, our faith grows so we can trust Him for greater things. Remember, Jesus was God in the flesh, the "Magnificent Lineman" and the reigning King. He links us with Divine resources sufficient for anything we face, *if we will only believe His promises and do His word*

11
Roadblock #2 – Sin

God hates sin and will have none of it in His heaven that is a kingdom where the will of the King is upheld. It will be for those who have settled this matter and have chosen to submit to God's authority and obey His will as their conscience and the light of Scripture have guided them. They will still battle with sin as Paul tells in Romans 7, but their will is to obey.

Let us remember how sin came about. God commanded our ancestors not to eat of a particular tree and warned them of the consequences that they would die if they did. Let us observe Satan's tactics to tempt them. He casts doubts about what God had really told them and gets Eve to question what God said. Then he undercuts the consequences of sin: "You will not surely die" (Gen. 3:4). That was enough. She saw how appealing the fruit seemed to be, so now doubting God's command and the consequences, sin entered the world and things have never been the same.

Satan has used since then the appealing fruit of sex tempting people to enjoy this apart from the biblical restraint until marriage. God made us male and female intending man and woman to commit for life in marital union and enjoy sexual relations there. Children would then have parents sharing the responsibility of raising them. Satan continued his strategy of getting us to look away from God's word in Scripture resulting in fornication, adultery, unwanted pregnancies, abortions, and homosexuality. Satan undermined the family unit God designed in creation leaving behind a trail of suffering.

Our world is out of control because it has ignored God's commands and the consequences of sin. Sometimes Christians are no different than the world about them and that ought to clue us something is very wrong. We are playing games in our Christian lives until we get serious about turning from sin. John the Baptist sounded the clarion call to repent and follow Jesus. The New Testament says we are predestined to be like Him, and Jesus clearly was different from the world and avoided sin like the plague. Until we settle this matter, sin will constitute a roadblock keeping us from discoveries made by the apostolic generation, as we shall see in this book.

God took a great risk when He, the Creator of all things, gave us the free will to choose either to obey or disobey Him, the Almighty God. His recourse was to ban us from His Presence and heaven where all obey, love, serve, worship Him, and live together in peace as members of His family. All who respond to the gospel and walk this kingdom way of turning from sin and obeying and serving Jesus as Lord are heading toward that destiny that God planned for us from the very beginning.

12

Roadblock #3 — Ignorance of the Word

Graphe is the Greek word for Scripture meaning the written word. *Logos,* also meaning "word," refers to the correct interpretation given by the Holy Spirit as we read today the written word He inspired in the first place. Jesus makes this difference clear in John 5. He said the Pharisees read the Scripture (*graphe*) diligently and yet they did not have the word (*logos*) in them. Without the Holy Spirit's help, the Pharisees then and people now are not able to understand the *logos* contained in the written word of Scripture.

In the earlier days of my disciple venture, I had a hang-up about the blood of Christ. When the Lord saw I was serious about walking in His way, then the Holy Spirit revealed the *logos* from Scripture regarding what Jesus did for me at the Cross. The written word came alive. Until then, I did not have a clue about what Scripture meant when it spoke of the importance of the blood Jesus shed for me. When I was ready and needed to know, then the Holy Spirit opened my spiritual eyes to see the *logos* of God's wonderful grace.

The Bible will come alive if you make the disciple venture described in the New Testament beginning with John the Baptist's call to repent and follow Jesus. Like the first converts, devote yourself to the apostles' teaching, fellowship, breaking of bread, and prayer (Acts 2:42). The Spirit was teaching them to huddle with Jesus from the first. Then, serve Jesus in the ministries to which He calls you and witness to your faith in Him in the world, unashamed in public to identify with Jesus. Practice such New Testament discipleship and the Holy Spirit will enable you to hear more of the *logos* as you read Scripture. Be ready to share your faith, but be on guard against pride or boasting of your knowledge of Scripture or your church's doctrine. Humility marks the pathway of true disciples of Jesus Christ.

I doubt if many of you could identify one thing done by Rome's first seven Caesars, much less their names. Yet, from that same period in time, you could tell me some of the deeds done by and have read the writings of two Jewish fishermen from Galilee and one Jewish Pharisee, all who became disciples of Jesus. The writings of Peter, John, and Paul comprise 21 of the 27 writings of the New Testament. Why are its writings so important? Why have they been circulated, read, and studied throughout the intervening centuries? Very simply, its Spirit-inspired witness tells how to walk with the Lord as the Lord of heaven Himself taught His apostles. We learn of blessings attending this pathway, its climax on earth, and eternal life with God forever in heaven. Study it, meditate on it, and memorize it, doing and believing the *logos* that the Holy Spirit reveals to you from Scripture.

13

The Teacher

Jesus was the prophet who spoke the word of the Lord regarding the New Covenant, as Moses was the prophet who spoke the word of the Lord about the Old Covenant. Jesus was Himself the Word (*logos*) because He was the Lord of heaven incarnate in human flesh.

Before His death, Jesus told His followers that after He returned to the Father, He would send the Holy Spirit who would teach them in the future. Jesus had so much more He wanted to tell them, but they could not handle it then. The Holy Spirit would bring to mind what Jesus taught, help them remember things they were not ready to understand, and then learn other things they needed to know. The Holy Spirit would teach them all this and more and inspire the writings they would leave for future generations so they could make the same discoveries leading to victory over sin, evil, and death.

No teacher since then or in the future will ever go beyond what Jesus and the Holy Spirit taught and the apostolic generation experienced as a result of the Incarnation and Return of Jesus. The ultimate possible in this life was revealed and experienced back then. That is why the doctrine of any church should be continually examined by succeeding generations with the Holy Spirit's guidance to see that it is in harmony with Scripture.

The Holy Spirit is not only the Teacher but also the Sanctifier. As we conform to His teaching, He forms the Christlike nature in us. The Holy Spirit led the first converts to devote themselves to four spiritual disciplines the first of which was the teaching of the apostles followed by fellowship, breaking of bread, and prayers. These spiritual disciplines helped the faithful make the kingdom journey and grow to maturity.

The Reformation recognized the New Testament as normative. This renewed focus, however, never took the church, for the most part, to the climax of Christian faith and experience discovered by the apostles during the days of Jesus' Return. This is revealed in such New Testament writings as Ephesians, Colossians, Hebrews, 2 Timothy, 2 Peter, 1 John, and James. In these days when Islam is spreading, it is time for the church to clarify the original faith and experience reported in the New Testament.

God uses spiritually gifted teachers to help us understand Scripture. When you hear different interpretations, check with trusted Christian friends, teachers, and pastors for insight. Then pray and go to the authoritative text of the Scripture and to the infallible teacher of the Holy Spirit who helps us to understand the *logos* of Scripture.

14

The New Temple

Paul taught that God was building a new temple during the days of the New Covenant. Unlike the old stone temple at Jerusalem during the days of the Old Covenant, this new temple, the Body of Christ, consisted of every believer responding to the Good News. They were connected with Jesus the Head of the Body and other members of the Body through the indwelling Holy Spirit. They formed a new living temple where God could dwell by His Spirit and continue the work of Jesus in the world.

Paul tells us in Ephesians that this Body or temple is built through the work of ministry as members use their spiritual gifts in dependence upon the Holy Spirit and guided by Jesus, the Head of the Body. Paul says one of the reasons for this work of ministry and building this living temple of the Body of Christ is so the Holy Spirit can bring members to completion according "to the measure of the stature of the fullness of Christ" (Eph 4:13). In other words, God wants to make Jesus' disciples into Christlike people.

Solomon's stone temple at Jerusalem was the focal point of the Old Covenant from the 10th to the 6th century B.C. The presence of the Lord dwelt there over the Ark of the Covenant made possible by the sacrifice of animals to atone for sin. That temple and the two that followed were all destroyed by A.D. 70 as the Old Covenant ended. The new temple of the Body of Christ and the New Covenant are eternal. The Holy Spirit dwells in the heart of each believer comprising that new temple because of Jesus' sacrifice to atone for all sin, for all people, for all time.

We need to stay connected with other Christians in this living temple of the Body of Christ. Here we receive nurture through the ministry of the word, Baptism, and the Lord's Supper. We are lifted by its prayers, helped through fellowship with like-minded believers, and hear Jesus call us to ministry. Just as arms, legs, and other parts need to remain connected to the body to stay alive, so must we who belong to Jesus Christ. Such fellowship with other believers helps us grow in Christ and remain fruitful preparing us to take our place someday with them in heaven as part of God's family.

Jesus, the Head of the Body of Christ, is the Lord worshiped in this new temple. Unlike the old stone temple, this New Covenant temple offers Christ hands and feet to carry on His work of ministry and lips to witness to the truth of God's amazing grace. We can see the wisdom of God's strategy in His covenantal activity planning for that future day when the whole earth will be filled with the knowledge of the Lord.

15
The Name

I don't have any facts at hand, but I wonder how much is done in the church today with little or no prayer. In other words, how many sermons, church school lessons, small groups, counseling sessions, etc. are done simply on human strength and wisdom? Little prayer means little Holy Spirit activity and that means little God power. The attendance decline in mainline churches means something is missing. The early church spread throughout the Roman world in one generation exhibiting a power clearly lacking in much of the church today. Jesus told His first followers to wait in prayer before the Lord until the Holy Spirit came upon them with the power they would need to follow Jesus in His kingdom way and carry on their ministry.

Power was released through the Name of Jesus to deliver people from spiritual bondage, heal the sick, overcome obstacles, and provide whatever was needed to carry on the work of witness and service. If we make this kingdom revolution journey, we shall find ourselves involved in spiritual warfare. Prayer also links us with the power to overcome such spiritual foes described by Paul in Ephesians 6:12 as principalities, powers, rulers of the darkness of this age, and spiritual hosts of wickedness in heavenly places. They get into our minds with thoughts to tempt us, fears to undermine our faith, and distractions to turn our attention away from Jesus and walking this way He pioneered before us.

God's power available through the Name is sufficient for whatever difficulties or spiritual warfare we may encounter.

The more we pray, the more the Spirit will lead us to give thanks to God for His grace and answers to prayer. The more we grow in Christ, the more the Spirit will lead us to praise the Lord. Such worship which Jesus said His Father yearned for will be freely given in heaven and emerge more in our lives as we grow closer to Christ. We shall increasingly come to value "the Name" and worship the One who bears it with thanksgiving and praise.

The church has the message the world needs and access to the power to make it happen. God needs kingdom revolution disciples who will partner with Him in prayer. One of the spiritual disciplines in Acts 2:42 to which the first Christians devoted themselves was prayer, enabling the early church to appropriate the power of the Holy Spirit. Beginning among the Jews and moving into the Gentile Roman world, Christianity spread despite all the hostile opposition. What would happen today if we made the same kingdom journey taught by Jesus and called upon His Name for the power to carry on the Father's work begun by Jesus and His apostles? I wonder!

16
Walking with the Lord

During the decade of the sixties when I encountered Christ, my heart was cleansed and the Spirit released. The Bible came alive as God's word and I saw Jesus clearly as the unique God/man. I was drawn to read the Gospels with a hunger to learn about Jesus whom I now saw as God living in our midst. Influenced by this reading of the Gospels and a devotional classic *Abide in Christ* by Andrew Murray, it became clear that "walking with the Lord" was at the center of the apostolic faith and experience. God intended the Christian life to be a "Journey with Jesus," the close relationship God wanted from the first.

The Lord of heaven came to earth and called twelve men to become His disciples. For three years they walked and talked with Him learning how God wanted us to live. Like branches connected to a vine, so His followers learned to connect with Him as they lived in this sinful world. John in his First Epistle says that the focal point of the Holy Spirit's counsel is that we abide in Jesus, and Jesus assured them He would abide in them. Huddling with Jesus by spending time in prayer and reading Scripture helps us to hear Him speak as we develop an intimate walk with the One to whom we are betrothed.

We tend to become like people we associate with over a long period of time. When you and I learn to walk with Jesus in fellowship with other like-minded disciples, we become like Him growing in righteousness and holiness with an increasing desire to turn from all sin and honor God. We grow in our desire to love God, serve Him as He calls, and share His love with others. This enables us to be makers of the peace in the world about us.

God has wanted people to walk with Him from the beginning. In the first twenty generations of biblical history, three men walked with God: Enoch, Noah, and Abraham. It was also said of Noah he obeyed God in all God commanded him. God brought the flood and began again on earth with Noah and his family. Abraham was an extraordinary man walking with God in faith and obedience. God covenanted with Abraham to bless him and eventually all peoples of the earth through one of his descendants. Paul said this was Jesus who blessed His followers with the Holy Spirit. It is clear from Scripture that God wants people who will walk with Him.

How can two walk together unless they agree? It is impossible. God will never agree to walk our sinful ways, so if we wish to walk with Him, we must repent and agree to walk God's way. The New Testament reports how to do this through the apostles who learned from Jesus and the Holy Spirit.

17

The Climax at the King's Return

Where does Isaiah's Highway of Holiness lead, this kingdom way Jesus taught and lived? It would take the faithful to heaven from which Jesus had come. All that had been lost back at the beginning as a result of sin would be regained through Jesus' Crucifixion, Resurrection, and Return. Let us look at what we lost down here as a result of our sin.

First, we were *alienated* from the Divine Presence. God wanted fellowship with us and designed us for that, but we lost this through sin. For such a relationship to work, we must learn submission and obedience to the Creator. Because of our sin, we were banished from the Divine Presence.

Second, we were *corrupted* as sin damaged the image of God in which we were made. Created to be like God, do the right, love others, and be holy, the first sin led to an ever-expanding corruption of life on this earth. Genesis reports prior to the flood that "the wickedness of man was great in the earth, and that every intent of the thoughts of his heart was only evil continually" (Gen. 6:5).

Third, we *died* spiritually and then physically. God said in the day you eat of the forbidden fruit, you will die. That referred to the spiritual death resulting from being disconnected from God and the corruption of the image of God within that would follow.

Years later, they died physically when they became disembodied spirits.

Jesus began the restoration by His Crucifixion, Resurrection, giving the Holy Spirit, and making the New Covenant. Jesus ended the alienation as He reconciled us to the Father by dying for our sin and then betrothed us to Himself. He overcame the corruption by breathing into His followers the Holy Spirit who began the sanctifying process creating new people after the lost image of God. Jesus conquered death by rising from the dead and giving His disciples the same hope of being raised from the dead at Jesus' Return.

This beginning restoration would be completed at the Return of Jesus. Those who walked faithfully with the Lord would be ready. At His Coming, Jesus would join Himself to the faithful as His bride. The Holy Spirit would complete the Christlike nature in them. Then the Lord would take them to heaven, giving them a new body like His resurrection body. All that had been lost through sin would be regained and more as a result of God's grace poured out to us through Jesus Christ.

18

Signs Marking the Time of Jesus' Return

During the last week of His life, Jesus told His disciples the temple would be destroyed in the future. Having been under His teaching for three years, they realized the gravity of this and that it was related to the last days, so they began to ask Him. "What will be the sign of your coming, and of the end of the age?" (Matt. 24:3)

The apocalyptic chapters of Matthew 24, Mark 13, and Luke 21 report Jesus' teaching on this subject. He told them there would be earthquakes, famines, plagues, wars, and rumors of wars. His followers would be persecuted and many martyred. Prior to the temple's destruction, an evil presence foretold by the prophet Daniel would take over this holy place where God had been worshiped for centuries. Blasphemies and abominations would fill it during those last days. Jesus exhorts the faithful to rejoice in the midst of all this tribulation because their redemption would be drawing near. He was referring to His Return when they would receive the promised reward.

There were earthquakes and famines. Tacitus and Suetonius report a massive plague around A.D. 65. Christian persecution began in A.D. 64 by the Roman Emperor Nero. One way to write "Nero Caesar" in Hebrew adds up to 666. There were wars and rumors of wars beginning in A.D. 66 as Jews and Gentiles turned against each other throughout the area. The corruption of the worship of God at the temple in Jerusalem began in A.D. 67–68 as zealots killed the priests in charge and took over at the temple. Blasphemies toward God, His Name, and abominations foretold by Daniel and Revelation all took place, well documented by Josephus.

Jesus knew His Crucifixion was near when He gave these signs about His Return. His disciples would face similar hostile opposition during those last days in the future resulting in their persecution and martyrdom. During His last night with them according to John 14, Jesus told them He was returning to the Father from whom He had come. He would prepare places for them in heaven and in the future would return so they could be with Him there in His Father's presence. The signs would alert them for when His Return was about to occur. Those signs began to be fulfilled about thirty years later.

Remember, Jesus gave these signs not for generations hundreds and thousands of years in the future, but for His disciples who had asked Him: "What will be the sign of Your coming and of the end of the age?" The purpose of the signs was to let them know when Jesus was about to return so they would be ready to deal with all the suffering and persecution awaiting them, and remain faithful.

19

Paul Expects Jesus' Return during Their Generation

Jesus' Crucifixion happened around A.D. 33 and we see about twenty years later that faith in Jesus' Return is still alive. From the very beginning in his ministry, Paul taught believers Jesus would return during their lifetime to bring the promised reward. In his earliest Letter of 1 Thessalonians, Paul assures them their loved ones who have died in the Lord will be raised from the dead at Jesus' Return. In fact, they will rise first. "Then we who are alive and remain shall be caught up together with them in the clouds to meet the Lord in the air" (4:17). Note that Paul includes himself in the "we who are alive and remain." Some will have fallen asleep or died and some will still be alive. In the next verse, Paul tells the Christians there in Thessalonica to comfort one another with these great words of hope as he writes this letter around the year A.D. 50.

Paul says in 1 Corinthians 15 written in the mid-fifties that Jesus will return and the dead will be raised *during their generation*. Some will still be alive at the trumpet. "Behold, I tell you a mystery: We shall not all sleep (meaning "we shall not all die"), but we shall all be changed–in a moment, in the twinkling of an eye, at the last trumpet" (1 Cor. 15:51–52). Note again that Paul includes himself among the "we" who will still be alive when the trumpet sounds. Paul tells in verse 52 that this is the trumpet when "the dead will be raised incorruptible, and we shall be changed." Paul comforts the Corinthians as He did the Thessalonians. In the midst of the persecution ahead for Christians, Jesus will return and raise the dead first. After that, He will remove the faithful from earth and they will join the ones who were first raised from the dead.

Some people were telling the Thessalonians in the early fifties that the Lord had already come. Paul says that is not true and reminds them how he told them about a special sign that will let them know when Jesus is about to return. Jesus had told His disciples about this same sign. At the temple in Jerusalem where sacrifices, prayers, and worship had been offered for years, powers of evil would take over (2 Thess. 2:3–4) bringing abominations and blasphemies. That would begin in A.D. 67–68 letting them know for certain the wait was over, Jesus' Return was truly at hand.

This is about the only time that Paul refers to signs about Jesus' Return in his letters. His pastoral concern focused on preparing his converts to be faithful so they would be ready for that Return whenever the exact day would be in their future. When Paul uses the pronoun "we" in these letters, he refers to himself and the Christians at Thessalonica and Corinth back in the first century, A.D., not persons two thousand years later. He clearly says not all will have yet slept or died, but some of them will still be alive when the trumpet sounds and the dead are raised during the days of Jesus' Return. Twenty years after Jesus' Crucifixion and Resurrection, the faith in Jesus' Return for their generation is still alive.

20

The Long Awaited Time Finally Arrives

Jesus came to earth from His Father in heaven and taught His first followers He would return for them in the future and take them also into the Father's presence. During His earthly ministry, Jesus said He did not know the exact time for the Second Coming, but it would be during their lifetime. About thirty years later, the Father tells Jesus the time is at hand for those events. Jesus sends an angel who reveals to John the second-coming events. He tells us this as he begins the Revelation. "The Revelation of Jesus Christ, which God gave Him to show His servants what must soon take place" (Rev. 1:1 NIV). John tells us in the next verse that Jesus sent His angel to reveal to John what the Father had revealed to Him. I believe John received the Revelation in A.D. 63.

Through two reliable witnesses, an angel and Jesus, we learn about God the Father's witness that the Return of Jesus was about to take place. Jesus confirms the accuracy of this testimony as He repeats three times at the end of the Revelation "I am coming soon." He also told His followers while on earth that some of them would still be alive to see "the Son of Man coming in His kingdom" (Matt. 16:28). That time had now come. At the end of the Revelation, the angel confirms the accuracy of his earlier testimony to John as he now tells John not to "seal the words of the prophecy of this book, for the time is at hand" (Rev. 22:10). Six centuries earlier, an angel told Daniel to seal up his vision about the last days because "it refers to many days in the future" (Dan. 8:26). What was off in the distant future for Daniel had arrived for John and his generation.

Here we have the testimony of God the Father, God the Son, an angel, and the apostle John. They all agreed Jesus would return back then. This witness is confirmed in the late letters of the New Testament. Paul writes to the Hebrews: "For yet a little while, and He who is coming will come and will not tarry" (Heb. 10:37). James writes: "Establish your hearts, for the coming of the Lord is at hand" (James 5:8). Peter writes, "The end of all things is at hand" (1 Peter 4:7). John, in addition to the Revelation, writes in one of his epistles: "Little children, it is the last hour; and as you have heard that the Antichrist is coming, even now many antichrists have come; by which we know it is the last hour" (1 John 2:18).

I don't think you can make it any clearer. There can be no doubt that the writers of these letters believed Jesus' Return was about to happen. The days of waiting were over. The news that the time had arrived was initiated by the Godhead and John takes care to convey the important information to believers back then so they will be ready.

21

What the Apostles Discovered

Paul led converts up the highway of holiness with a passion to know Jesus Christ to whom they had been betrothed. Paul says in Philippians 3 that he has surrendered all things to Christ and is eagerly expecting to be completed and know the power of the Resurrection. Such surrender is the key to receiving such revelation. Jesus said the pure in heart shall see God.

In Revelation 10:7, an angel tells John that a mystery foretold by the prophets of old would be fulfilled at the seventh trumpet. In Ephesians 1:9; 3:3, 4, 9; 5:32; 6:19 and Colossians 1:26–27; 2:2; 4:3, Paul now talks about how a mystery has been revealed to the apostles and prophets. I believe this is the same mystery as he now talks about the fulfillment of earlier second-coming expectations.

At the beginning of his ministry, Paul said the hearts of the faithful would be established blameless in holiness when Jesus returned (1 Thess. 3:13). In other words, the faithful would be completed, perfected, or have the Christlike nature formed within at the Second Coming. Hebrews 11:40 says this would occur together with the Old Testament heroes of the faith such as Noah, Abraham, and Moses. Hebrews 12:23 reports that such persons existed when that epistle was written as it refers to the "spirits of just men made perfect." This was now the focus of Paul's ministry as we see in his later letters. He wrote to the Colossians how he devotes all his energy to "present every man perfect in Christ Jesus" (Col. 1:28).

Paul talks in Ephesians and Colossians about how resurrection power has now raised the faithful before the throne (Eph 2:6; Col 2:12; 3:1). He also speaks in Ephesians 5:31–32 about how the faithful among the betrothed have been joined in spiritual union with Jesus as part of a great mystery, like the union of a man and woman in marriage. *Such things are indeed a mystery, needing revelation.* Paul prays to that end for the Ephesians in 1:17.

I like to refer to the above as the experiential dimension of the Second Coming in contrast to its cosmic dimension. The latter refers to those one-time events such as Jesus beginning to reign, punishing the powers of evil, and terminating the Old Covenant; the former refers to what the faithful discovered when Jesus returned and is ongoing in nature, open to all future generations.

It is beyond the scope of this book to go into detail about the above that raises many questions. More details about what the apostles discovered during those days of Jesus' Return are found in *Bringing Heaven to Earth Because He Has Returned*. See "One Final Note" at the end of Appendix 3 for a description of this book.

22

Old Ages End and a New
Eternal Day Dawns

Paul wrote to the Corinthians that we are those "on whom the ends of the ages have come" (1 Cor. 10:11). Several ages ended during the days Jesus returned. One was the age of the Old Covenant. Paul refers in Hebrews 8:13 to the Old Covenant as "becoming obsolete and growing old" and "ready to vanish away." That happened as the temple and city were destroyed in A.D. 70.

In a sense, the world that the Jews had known came to an end in A.D. 70. Prior to that, they were the only nation on earth who had ever been in covenant with God and have God's kingdom dwell among them. Now after Jesus and His death to atone for sin, the New Covenant people consisted of anyone on earth who responded to the gospel, whether Jew or Gentile. The kingdom and its resources were no longer tied to one nation as during the days of the Old Covenant, but now open to disciples from any nation.

The age of Satan's authority over this earth gained because of sin came to an end when Jesus returned and at the seventh trumpet: "The kingdoms of this world have become the kingdoms of our Lord and of His Christ, and He shall reign forever and ever!" (Rev. 11:15) Bondage to death likewise ended as Jesus raised the dead to eternal life during those last days.

The age of the promises to Abraham had been fulfilled. God blessed his descendants as He promised. He gave them a land and made them a great nation. Unfortunately, they broke covenant and God made a New Covenant in which He fulfilled one last promise to Abraham. One of his descendants would take the blessing of Abraham to all nations. Paul, in Galatians 3:13–14, identified Jesus as that descendant and the Holy Spirit as the blessing.

The period of the authority of Daniel's four nations, Babylon, Media–Persia, Greece, and Rome, also ended as the kingdom came into the hands of Jesus during the Roman period. A new earth resulted as Jesus now ruled in place of Satan. Jesus also now reigned over the kingdom of God in this world where its treasures and miracles may be discovered and appropriated in the Nation of Christianity. A new heaven also existed as the dead were raised and humans occupied their place in heaven for the first time.

A new eternal day dawned on earth when these ages ended at Jesus' Return. Things were now in place so God could work toward the grand climax of peace on earth. He had provided what was beyond our ability to do anything about by overcoming sin, death, and the powers of evil. Now He would need faithful disciples to follow Jesus in His kingdom revolution, serve the reigning King who works to make all things new, and advance His cause on this earth.

23

Between Jesus' Return and History's Grand Finale

The church must get beyond the second-coming barrier and begin to live in the period between the Second Coming and history's grand finale. Two biblical passages talk about this period: 1 Corinthians 15:20-28 and Isaiah 2:2–4. The latter also tells what must transpire to reach history's climax.

Paul talks in the above Corinthian text about three distinct events in God's salvation history. First, the Resurrection of Jesus from the dead, second, Jesus' Return or Second Coming when He began His reign and raised His people from the dead, and third, the end of all history when Jesus will give the kingdom He received at the Second Coming back to God the Father so that the Father may be all things to all people. This "end" is not the Second Coming to which Paul has just previously referred. This end results from Jesus' reign over all things that only began at the Second Coming when the dead were first raised. After many years of Jesus' reign, then every "rule, authority and power" will be subject to Him leading to God's desired conclusion.

Isaiah's vision in 2:2–4 begins with the Second Coming as he refers to the "latter days" when Zion is established as the highest of the mountains. This would happen at the trumpet when its King, the Jewish Messiah Jesus, begins His reign over this earth from the heavenly, not the earthly, Mt. Zion as Hebrews

12:22–23 makes clear. This Hebrews text tells us during those days when Jesus was returning, the faithful on earth drew near to the heavenly Jerusalem, angels in festal gathering, the church of the first born, and the spirits of righteous men made perfect. The scene on the earthly Mt. Zion and Jerusalem was one of warfare that would end with Roman armies destroying the city and temple as the Old Covenant ended. Isaiah then looks ahead to history's grand finale when the nations of the earth learn war no more and live in peace with one another. During this time between the Second Coming and the end of history, Jesus reigns over this world from the heavenly Mt. Zion.

Isaiah then describes God's strategy to bring peace to the earth. The peoples of the earth must come to this God of Zion, learn His ways, *and finally do them.* Updating this to the period after the Lord's Incarnation and Return, the gospel must spread throughout the entire world with more and more people becoming disciples of Jesus, learning God's way, and putting it into practice. The church must stop waiting for Jesus' Return with the belief that He will then bring peace. Jesus did return and God put in place all that is needed to put this world together. He requires and needs our cooperation to work with the reigning King. This joint effort will result in God's grand finale, peace on earth.

24

A Further Look at God's Strategy

God knew He had to come down to this earth and get involved in this broken world if there would be any hope. There have been three temples according to Scripture indicating where the Lord dwelt on earth and how He got involved down here. Each Christian is vitally involved in the third temple.

First, the Lord entered into the Old Covenant with the Israelites during the days of Moses and dwelt over the Ark among the people. He delivered them from Egyptian slavery, brought them through the wilderness into the Promised Land, and into the glory days during the reign of David and Solomon. After dwelling with them over the Ark of the Covenant from the days of Moses with the mobile tent through the days of Solomon's temple prior to its destruction, the Lord departed because the people broke covenant.

The second member of the Godhead came down about six centuries later and took on mortal flesh in the miracle of the Incarnation, appearing as Jesus, our Emmanuel (God with us). Jesus referred to His body as a temple on one occasion. While Jesus' ministry focused on reaching the Jewish people, the significance of His Crucifixion and Resurrection were of such importance that the resultant New Covenant was opened to all people, Jews and Gentiles. This eternal covenant provided all we needed through the forgiveness of sins and the gift of the Holy Spirit to build a living relationship with God and loving relationships with one another, necessary to someday have peace on this earth.

God's strategy now shifted from the Jewish people alone to all people. Through the New Covenant, God was building a new temple in this world to house the third member of the Godhead, the Holy Spirit. Paul says this temple consists of each Christian in Ephesians 2:21-22. In contrast to Solomon's stone temple, this new temple would now give God hands, feet, and lips to carry on His work over all this earth through His people. Everything needed to reach the entire world was now in place, *but requiring the cooperation of His people.*

In this new day, we see His strategy in Jesus' last words to His followers: "You will be my witnesses...to the ends of the earth" (Acts 1:8 NIV). God needs His people throughout the whole world to spread the good news of His love. We do that through kind deeds and witnessing words about what Jesus means to us. He needs both. If our lips are silent, then we get the credit for our kind deeds as others say what nice people we are. Witness about what Jesus means to our lives enables God to get the credit. Such testimony combined with kind deeds has great drawing power to help God reach the world for Christ.

25

Claiming the Earth for Christ

Imagine a large slum tenement owned by an evil landlord who cares nothing for the people except to exploit them. Some want to improve things, but give up with no cooperation from the landlord. Others, like the landlord, care nothing about the state of the tenement, fighting with their neighbors and destroying the surroundings. Their plight remains hopeless as long as its evil landlord manages it. Suppose one day a beneficent landlord with limitless resources buys the tenement intending to invest himself and his resources in the people and the building. He shares his dream about the new apartments and sets guidelines for the behavior he expects.

Let us note one fact. A new day dawns at the very time when the beneficent landlord takes control. Nothing seems different, but to those who learn about the change in management and the new manager's plans, it is a new day. Prior to that moment, all was hopeless. Individual efforts to improve were futile. Under the new manager who desires to repair the tenement, help the people, and possesses the authority and resources to accomplish the task, a new day has indeed dawned. The new landlord needs only time to share the vision and enlist the cooperation of the tenants.

Our planet was like that slum tenement prior to the Incarnation and the Return of Jesus. Under the management of an evil landlord, Satan, called in Scripture a "liar" and "destroyer,"

49

the prophetic dream of peace was impossible. The best human efforts availed little against the powers of darkness organized for destruction. After the seventh trumpet, when God gave to Jesus Christ the authority to govern this world, peace becomes possible on this new earth through the new government of Him who works to "make all things new" (Rev. 21:5). Now He needs us to be there for Him, taking our marching orders from the Lord and not the world.

Make no mistake about it. Moving from where we are to peace on earth, kingdom disciples will be caught up in the eternal struggle between God and Satan; however, we can now prevail. Jesus needs us growing in a faith rooted in scriptural promises, seeking His glory and not our own, praying for direction to know His will, and praying for His power to win the battle. "The battle is not yours, but God's" (2 Chron. 20:15). "The Lord will fight for you" (Exod. 14:14). God spoke thus to His people facing impossible situations in the past. They depended on God and He fought for them. He will also fight for kingdom disciples today who seek to advance His cause through witness and service, turning their part of the world right side up.

26

The Banner Leading the Way
to the Grand Finale

Jesus, His word, and His kingdom, this is the banner I would like to raise for the church. He has come, returned, and reigns. We have His word that tells us how to appropriate His kingdom and its treasures. If Islamic terrorists can be inspired by hate to make great sacrifices for their cause, how much more ought we who belong to Jesus who died for our sin go all out to reach the world for Christ, whose kingdom cause promises such a grand finale.

My wife and I visited the Butchart Gardens in Victoria, British Columbia. Originally, it was a gaping wound in the earth's surface, an abandoned limestone quarry. The wife of the owner had a vision of what it could become with hard work and investment. It has now been converted into this beautiful scenic garden filled with flowers of all kinds and colors along with shrubs, fountains, etc. Attracting over a million visitors each year, it all began with a vision by Mrs. Butchart, wife of the owner, to convert the scarred earth into a beautiful garden.

God gave through the prophets a beautiful vision of a world where people will someday live in peace. The Garden of Eden where God dwelt at the beginning gave way to a spiritual wasteland because of sin and evil. God sent Jesus to show and teach the way on how to get our lives right and then put the world together. He needs faithful disciples and servants who follow His example and live by His word. They sow the kingdom seeds of love and righteousness that will someday produce a harvest of peace on our earth, the beautiful garden God intended from the beginning.

Upon hearing I believed the Second Coming had happened, a young woman responded: "What is there to look forward to then?" Everything! It means we live in a world where Jesus reigns and peace is possible and we can invest our lives for the greatest cause ever. It means we do not have to go through the terrible three-and-one-half-year tribulation period when evil powers were given authority over the peoples of the earth, even Christians. It means if we walk faithfully with Jesus, we shall join the faithful of the apostolic and subsequent generations who never died. We shall transition at once to the glorified body and live forever with the Lord in heaven.

God waits for us to return to the New Testament, learning and living by His word, and thereby enabling the reigning king to bring heaven to this earth. This will happen as Christians refocus on Jesus, His word, and His kingdom and *recover the faith and experience of the apostles from its beginning to its climax.* There is no other way. Let's go for it! Yes! Amen!

27

How Should I Think about the Second Coming?

After two thousand years of failed predictions, I find that many Christians have grown indifferent about the Second Coming. We can understand why this is so. Not only does mystery surround the events, but also that important event of Jesus' Return just never seems to happen.

That was not the case for the apostolic generation. They believed Jesus was going to return at the conclusion of their lives on earth. They knew full well the significance of that important moment. They would give an account of how they lived in response to God's grace. This is an important aspect of New Testament Christianity that we need to recover today because it motivates us to live our best for Christ. That final evaluation is coming for all of us.

When people hear I believe the Second Coming already happened and yet look for the Return of Christ for me, they wonder what I mean. When you believe you live in a world where Jesus has returned, then you are looking forward to Him returning for you at the end of your life just as He did for the first Christians. Because of the promised reward, you seek to prepare your life for that climactic moment, as did those first Christians, by learning from the apostles what Jesus taught about how God wants His people to live. That is finally what life down here is all about in this world of people who rebelled against the Creator's plan and purpose for them.

When it has all been said and done and the records of our lives on earth are completed, it all comes down to this: Did we truly respond to God's offer of grace by becoming disciples of Jesus and walking in His ways? What will that final record of our lives show? Did we trust in His grace? Did we walk in the light of a good conscience, turning from sin when the Holy Spirit convicted us? Did we reach out to help the poor and needy, as we were able? Did we forgive others when they wronged us? Did we serve Christ as we had opportunity?

I would encourage each Christian to see the day you depart this earth as the day Jesus returns for you. Will you have prepared for that most important moment in your life? I find it motivates me to see that event in this light. God will not be looking at how much money, power, or fame we accumulated in this world. He will be looking at how we used His costly investment in us: the Cross to provide Atonement for sin, the gift of the Holy Spirit, and spiritual gifts for serving. Was He able to use our hands in serving others and doing deeds of kindness? Was He able to use our lips to speak of our faith and gratitude in His amazing love? Whatever it takes to motivate you to do your very best for Christ, do it. You want to have so lived for Him during your days on earth that Jesus will say to you on that day of accountability when you stand before Him: "Well done, good and faithful servant."

Appendix 1

SCRIPTURE INDICATES JESUS TO RETURN BACK THEN

Jesus' Witness while on Earth about His Future Return

"Behold, I will send you Elijah the prophet before the coming of the great and dreadful day of the Lord" (Mal. 4:5). Jesus said that John the Baptist was this person whose ministry would be a sign that the last days were near. "For all the prophets and the law prophesied until John. And if you are willing to receive it, he is Elijah who is to come" (Matt. 11:13–14).

"Assuredly, I say to you, there are some standing here who shall not taste death till they see the Son of Man coming in His kingdom" (Matt. 16:28).

"And this gospel of the kingdom will be preached in all the world as a witness to all the nations, and then the end will come" (Matt. 24:14). In one of Paul's late epistles, he says this has been fulfilled as he writes that the gospel "was preached to every creature under heaven" (Col. 1:23).

"Assuredly I say to you, this generation will by no means pass away till all these things are fulfilled" (Matt. 24:34).

Jesus' Witness from Heaven to John as His Return Was at Hand

"The revelation of Jesus Christ, which God gave Him to show His servants what must soon take place" (Rev. 1:1 NIV).

"Blessed is he who reads and those who hear the words of this prophecy, and keep those things which are written in it; for the time is near" (Rev. 1:3).

"Hold fast what you have till I come" (Rev. 2:25).

"I am coming soon. Hold on to what you have, so that no one will take your crown" (Rev. 3:11 NIV).

"Do not seal up the words of the prophecy of this book, for the time is at hand" (Rev. 22:10). About six centuries earlier, when Daniel received his visions about the last days, the angel told him "seal up the vision, for it refers to many days in the future" (Dan. 8:26). John is told to do exactly the opposite and the reason for this. The last days have come.

"Behold, I am coming soon! Blessed is he who keeps the words of the prophecy in this book" (Rev. 22:7 NIV).

"Behold, I am coming soon! My reward is with me, and I will give to everyone according to what he has done (Rev. 22:12 NIV).

"He who testifies to these things says, 'Yes, I am coming soon'" (Rev. 22:20 NIV).

The Testimony from the Acts of the Apostles and the Epistles

"And it shall come to pass in the last days, says God, that I will pour out My Spirit on all flesh; your sons and your daughters shall prophesy, your young men shall see visions, your old men shall dream dreams" (Acts 2:17).

"Now all these things happened to them as examples, and they were written for our admonition, on whom the ends of the ages have come" (1 Cor. 10:11).

"Behold, I tell you a mystery: We shall not all sleep, but we shall all be changed—in a moment, in the twinkling of an eye, at the last trumpet. For the trumpet will sound, and the dead will be raised incorruptible, and we shall be changed" (1 Cor. 15:51–52).

"Let us consider one another in order to stir up love and good works, not forsaking the assembling of ourselves together, as is the manner of some, but exhorting one another, and so much the more as you see the Day approaching" (Heb. 10:24–25).

"For yet a little while, and He who is coming will come and will not tarry" (Heb. 10:37).

"Establish your hearts, for the coming of the Lord is at hand" (James 5:8)

"Behold, the Judge is standing at the door!" (James 5:9)

"But the end of all things is at hand; therefore be serious and watchful in your prayers" (1 Pet. 4:7).

"Little children, it is the last hour; and as you have heard that the Antichrist is coming, even now many antichrists have come, by which we know that it is the last hour" (1 John 2:18).

"But you, beloved, remember the words which were spoken before by the apostles of our Lord Jesus Christ: how they told you that there would be mockers in the last time who would walk according to their own ungodly lusts" (Jude 17–18).

Appendix 2

SIGNS POINT TO HIS COMING BACK THEN

"Teacher, but when will these things be? And what sign will there be when these things are about to take place?" (Luke 21:7) "And what will be the sign of your coming, and of the end of the age?" (Matt. 24:3) Jesus had just told His disciples that the beloved temple, the center of the Old Covenant and Jewish worship, would be utterly destroyed. These Jewish disciples anxiously wanted to know when will such unbelievable desolation take place? Jesus proceeds to answer these questions by giving them what they asked: particular signs that would let them know when those days would be upon them. We read of these in the apocalyptic chapters of Matthew 24, Mark 13, and Luke 21.

Before looking at five of the signs Jesus gave His disciples on that Palm Sunday, we shall look at two other signs based on Old Testament prophecies that occurred at the beginning of the apostolic generation. The one took place just before Jesus began His ministry, and the other just after He completed His ministry. The next five signs are what Jesus told His disciples in response to their questions. These would begin to occur about thirty years later toward the end of their generation. The signs were never intended for unknown future generations but for His disciples and that generation who would pass through those events. The purpose of the signs was to alert them so they would not be caught off guard during those days of suffering and persecution, but prepared for that climax to their faith journey. All of the historical events referred to in the following are documented in the earlier book, *Bringing Heaven to Earth Because He Has Returned.*

Elijah the Prophet

"Behold, I will send you Elijah the prophet before the coming of the great and dreadful day of the Lord" (Mal. 4:5). This last book of the Old Testament reports one of the signs pointing to the generation to experience the last days. Elijah would appear on the scene. Jesus told His hearers about the new day dawning with the ministry of John the Baptist. "For all the prophets and the law prophesied until John" (Matt. 11:13). God was launching a new work that would result in a New Covenant of grace through the life, death, and Resurrection of the Jewish Messiah. Jesus continued in the next verse: "And if you are willing to receive it, he is Elijah who is to come" (Matt. 11:14). By identifying John the Baptist as the Elijah foretold in Malachi, Jesus was saying that "the dreadful day of the Lord" was in the future for that generation. John would prepare the way for Jesus, the Messiah, and at His Return, He would reward the faithful and bring judgment on the powers of evil and those who rejected God's offer of grace.

Pouring Out the Holy Spirit

The appearing of Elijah occurred just prior to the beginning of Jesus' ministry while this next sign foretold by Joel occurred just after His life, death, and Resurrection on the Day of Pentecost. The Spirit was poured out and His disciples began to speak in other tongues. Spectators were saying that they were simply drunk. The Spirit then leads Peter to address the crowd. He assures them that they are not drunk but that Joel's prophecy has just been fulfilled in their midst. "But this is what was spoken by the prophet Joel: 'And it shall come to pass in the last days, says God, that I will pour out My Spirit on all flesh...And on My menservants and on

60

My maidservants I will pour out My Spirit in those days; and they shall prophesy" (Acts 2:14–18). Peter continues to quote from Joel saying such a pouring out of the Spirit will precede the coming Day of the Lord and all who call on the Lord will be saved. Peter proclaimed the Good News that would prepare people for the coming day of judgment.

Peter clearly says that the pouring out of the Holy Spirit fulfilled the prophecy in Joel pointing to another sign that "the last days" were coming on their generation. *They were the ones.* Jesus knew that, so during that last week He was with them, He spoke of signs to look for so that they would know when finally the time had come. It would be about thirty years later during the decade of the sixties that the signs Jesus gave would begin to appear.

Persecution of Christians

Jesus foretold persecution for His followers when He returned during the last days. In Mark 13, Matthew 24, and Luke 21, Jesus describes the events associated with the Second Coming. "But before all these things, they will lay their hands on you and persecute you, delivering you to the synagogues and prisons, and you will be brought before kings and rulers for My name's sake" (Luke 21:12). The Lord revealed similar things to His first followers in the Revelation given to John. The powers of darkness would be given authority during the last days "to make war with the saints and to overcome them" (Rev. 13:7). This broke out against the first Christians at the end of the apostolic generation during the reign of the Roman Emperor Nero toward the latter part of A.D. 64. Tacitus describes the torturous deaths to which the first Christians were subjected. There have been other times of persecution for Christians in the intervening centuries, but the one related to Jesus' Return was during the reign of the Roman Emperor Nero.

Wars and Rumors of Wars

Jesus said there would be wars and rumors of wars during the days of His Return. Josephus reports about all the wars breaking out beginning in the year A.D. 66. Jewish zealots attack Masada and kill the Romans there and then stir up trouble at the temple in Jerusalem. These zealots slay Roman soldiers who had laid down their arms having been promised security, and on the very same day, the Caesarians rise up and kill the Jews occupying their city. This begins the wars between the Jews and their Gentile neighbors as they kill each other during the remainder of that decade. Cestius, a Roman officer, in retaliation for these attacks by the Zealots kills the Jews in a certain town who did not go down to the Feast of Booths at Jerusalem, and shortly thereafter, the zealots retaliate and inflict defeat upon Cestius. This would launch the Jews into war with the mighty Roman armies. It would be their last war during the days of the Old Covenant. Such "wars and rumors of wars" during the period A.D. 66–70 fulfilled another sign by Jesus indicating the last days were taking place at the conclusion of the apostolic generation.

Gospel Preached Throughout the World

In Matthew 24, Jesus taught about something that would be accomplished just before the end during the apostolic generation. All persons on earth would have had the opportunity to hear the Good News that He came to announce. "And this gospel of the kingdom will be preached in all the world as a witness to all the nations, and then the end will come" (Matt. 24:14). After His Crucifixion and Resurrection, Jesus told His disciples He would ascend to heaven and pour out the Holy Spirit empowering His followers to witness "in Jerusalem, and in all Judea and Samaria, and to the end of the earth" (Acts 1:8). He told the apostles they would take the gospel throughout the world. While others assisted in the spread of the gospel, God chose Paul as His primary spokesman to the Gentiles.

Writing near the end of his ministry, Paul makes an amazing statement in Colossians 1:23 that the gospel has been "preached to every creature under heaven." I have no idea how Paul understands this to have been accomplished. This text has opened the door for all kinds of interpretation to explain that Paul meant something other than what he said. When you believe the biblical witness that the Second Coming occurred during the apostolic generation, then it is not difficult to believe the witness of Paul at this point. At the time he wrote Colossians, God's spokesman to the Gentiles says "every creature under heaven" has heard the gospel fulfilling another sign indicating the last days were upon that generation.

Evil Presence Inhabits the Temple

Foretold by the Prophet Daniel, described by Jesus as "The Abomination that Makes Desolation," Paul spoke of this sign in 2 Thessalonians 2:1-5. Some at Thessalonica in the early fifties were saying Jesus had already returned. Paul says Jesus has not yet returned and reminds them how he had told them about this important sign that would let them know when those days were at hand. At that time, the temple would be filled with blasphemies toward the living God and His Name along with all kinds of evil. Zealots killed the duly appointed priests and appointed their own priests during this period of A.D. 67–70 and the corruption began. They were unaware of the evil presence that was using them to oppose the living God as recorded in prophecy. Jesus told His followers to flee Jerusalem when they see this sign. This would point to the imminent terrible last days associated with Jesus' Return when the temple and city would be destroyed. Josephus details the unbelievable abominations in that holy site where God had been worshiped for centuries. As prophesied, the temple was destroyed, animal sacrifices ended, and the Old Covenant came to an end.

Destruction of the Temple

The most readily observable sign pointing to the last days and the time of the Return of the Lord was the destruction of the temple at Jerusalem. Jesus told His disciples about this during His last week at the temple while He was still with them. During the days of the Old Covenant, the temple in Jerusalem was the center for the worship of God as well as the sacrifices to atone for sin that enabled God to dwell in their midst. The people broke covenant and God rendered judgment upon them through the Babylonians in the sixth century B.C. After returning them to their land, a few centuries later, the defining moment came. As Jesus entered Jerusalem on Palm Sunday, He knew the Jewish leaders had rejected Him and His death was imminent. Jesus told His disciples about the destruction of the temple and that happened during the period A.D. 67–70. During those last days, Jerusalem and its temple were destroyed ending forever the Old Covenant of law with its animal sacrifices. They were replaced with the everlasting New Covenant of grace with the sacrifice of Jesus on the Cross to atone for sin, open to all people, Jews and Gentiles.

Summary

Let me point out one thing in closing. Some of the signs Jesus gave regarding His Return can be repeated in history such as wars, plagues, and persecutions. Some of the above signs pointing to the Return of Jesus Christ will never happen again. There will never be another Elijah foretelling the great and dreadful day of the Lord. Jesus Himself said that John the Baptist was the "Elijah to come" marking that generation back then as the one to pass through those days of judgment. There will never be another Pentecost that marked the fulfillment of the prophecy in Joel. There will be other times when the Spirit is poured out, but the one indicating the last days were drawing near was clearly identified by Peter as what happened on Pentecost, again marking the apostolic generation as the time when those climactic events would occur. There will never be another temple to be destroyed at Jerusalem. What gave validity to those temples at Jerusalem from the time of Solomon to A.D. 70 was the Old Covenant along with the worship and atoning sacrifices offered there to God. Jesus said this was the temple to be destroyed during those last days. It was indeed destroyed at the end of the apostolic generation and the Old Covenant came to an end forever.

I have heard persons acknowledge that these signs have been fulfilled and then say that now we just have to wait for Jesus' Return. Remember, Jesus gave these signs in response to His disciples' questions as to when He would return. Jesus knew they were "the generation" and would be facing the onslaught of the powers of evil during those last days when many would be martyred. The signs were to alert them to an all out spiritual effort to be watchful, prayerful, and supportive of one another. "Now when these things begin to happen, look up and lift your heads, because your redemption draws near"(Luke 21:28). Luke wants to make clear that during those terrible last days of judgment, wrath, wars and rumors of wars, persecution, the destruction of the temple, and the end of the Old Covenant, their redemption would be drawing near, as Jesus would return with the promised reward for the faithful.

Appendix 3

MORE TO THINK ABOUT

In addition to the scripture verses and signs contained in the first two appendices pointing to Jesus' Return during the apostolic generation, this third appendix presents "more to think about" to show the basis for believing this concept which may be new for many of the readers.

What about the Return of Jews to Jerusalem in 1948?

Many believe the return of the Jews in 1948 was a sign pointing to the Second Coming of Jesus Christ. Let's clarify a bit of Jewish history. When the Jewish people broke covenant with God, He took the kingdom from them and removed them from the land for seventy years using the Babylonians for this disciplinary measure around the 6th Century B.C. When it came time to fulfill His promise to return the people to their land preparatory to the coming of the Messiah, God used the Medes and the Persians to free them from Babylonian captivity and help them return. They provided protection from their enemies and materials to rebuild the city and temple. That is the way the God of the Bible even during the days of the Old Covenant returned His people to their land after the period of judgment.

Think about It

Living in the days since the Messiah has come and revealed the
incredible compassion and grace of God as Jesus died on the Cross
for our sin, do you think in your wildest dreams that God would
plan to use a butcher like Hitler and his Holocaust to accomplish
a gracious act of returning the people to their land? I love the
Jewish people and am indebted to them for the faith I have in
Jesus Christ. However, history witnesses to the fact that with their
rejection of Jesus, Romans destroyed the temple, the city, and
removed the people from the land. The Old Covenant came to an
end. Since then, they have wandered over the earth facing endless
persecutions such as Hitler's Holocaust. Since A.D. 70, they have
not been in covenant with God nor had the covenantal benefit of
Atonement for sin. Their suffering servant of Isaiah 53 provided
that through the Cross and waits to welcome them home via the
New Covenant with all its blessings.

**What about Building Another Temple to Prepare for Jesus'
Return?**

The second-coming prophecies tell about the destruction of the
temple in Jerusalem when Jesus returned. This is a problem for
those who are looking for His Return any day now. There is no
temple. In the belief that the temple will one day in the future
be rebuilt on that location preparatory to the anticipated Second
Coming, I have heard that young men are being prepared to
once again re-institute animal sacrifice and preparations are being
made to quickly construct a temple.

Think about It

Why would God lead people to rebuild another stone temple and
offer animal sacrifices again when that Old Covenant failed? Jesus
as the Lamb of God made one sacrifice for all sin for all time by

dying on the Cross. God now operates in this world through the New Covenant made through the Jewish Messiah Jesus and open to all people. Frankly, it would be unthinkable for anybody to even approach the living God with animal blood at this point in history. Also, no temple rebuilt there would have any covenantal significance now. It was the Old Covenant that gave validity to the Jerusalem temple as well as the animal sacrifice practiced there to make Atonement for sin. That all ended in A.D. 70.

Who Were the People Who Would Never Die?

Jesus said to Martha shortly before raising her brother from the dead: "He who believes in Me, though he may die, he shall live. And whoever lives and believes in Me shall never die" (John 11:25-26) Who were these people Jesus said would never die? They were clearly part of the generation living on earth when Jesus returned. He would remove them from their bodies, give them the new glorified body, and take them to heaven.

From Adam on prior to Jesus' Return, people became disembodied spirits when they died entering a state of sleep, leaving their bodies on earth to decay. Scriptures seem to indicate that they were awakened from sleep at Jesus' Resurrection but not yet raised from the dead. Paul is clear that the dead would not be raised until the trumpet at Jesus' Return. "For the trumpet will sound, and the dead will be raised incorruptible" (1 Cor. 15:52). In the previous verse, he also said this would happen during their lifetime. "We shall not all sleep" until this climactic event occurs. Paul says in the earlier Epistle of 1 Thessalonians (4:16) that after the dead were raised first, Jesus would return with them to remove the faithful still alive on earth. These latter would be the first people who would never die. All the faithful since then will likewise never die, that is, become disembodied spirits, but rather discard this old body, receive the new glorified body, and live forever with the faithful of all ages in heaven. I have found that many Christians already believe this but are not aware that such a belief is dependent upon Jesus having returned back then.

Think about It

Jesus had to return back then because the apostles, who had been mentored by Jesus Himself, would surely have been among the people who "lived and believed," hence, a part of those who would never die. Peter, Paul, and John are such examples. They grew to maturity during that generation as the Holy Spirit formed the Christlike nature in them as attested in their New Testament writings. If Jesus did not return back then and the trumpet has not yet sounded when the dead are raised, then the apostles would have died after being transformed into the likeness of Christ and still not have their resurrection bodies. This would mean that Abraham, Isaac, Jacob, Moses, David, and Daniel who had already been waiting for as much as two thousand years would still be waiting. Add to that number all who died in the faith since the apostles, and at our death we would join that unfulfilled waiting throng. That does not square with the Revelation. The martyrs under the altar crying out to God in Revelation 6:10–11 asking how much longer they must wait for vindication are told just *a little while longer!* Hmmmm–2,000 years–a little while!

Why Are Bodies Still in the Graves if Jesus Has Returned?

One major point of confusion about believing that Jesus returned back in the first century is that the bodies are still in the graves. The apostle Paul answers this question. He writes in Philippians 3:20–21: "For our citizenship is in heaven, from which we also eagerly wait for the Savior, the Lord Jesus Christ, who will transform our lowly body that it may be conformed to His glorious body, according to the working by which He is able even to subdue all things to Himself." The word "transform" is a misleading translation. This is not the Greek word, *metamorphoo*, from which "metamorphosis" derives that would mean the old body is transformed into the new glorified body. The Greek word here is *metaschematidzo* and simply means to change the fashion or form of something without any necessity of a transformation. Paul uses this word in 2 Corinthians 11:13 to refer to false apostles appearing as apostles of Christ and again in 2 Corinthians 11:14 to refer to Satan appearing as an angel of light. Paul is simply saying in Philippians 3:20–21 that when the dead are raised, the form in which they are seen will be changed from the old physical body to the new glorified body. The old body was not transformed into the new glorified body any more than those false apostles were transformed into apostles of light or Satan was transformed into an angel of light. In other words, *metaschematidzo*, simply means that whereas they had lived on earth in a physical body, that form is changed to the glorified body when they are raised to heaven, not requiring any transformation of the physical body that is left in the grave.

Jesus' body was transformed as foretold in prophecy that God would not let His Holy One see corruption. No sin was ever found in Jesus and His Father did not let His body decay. It was transformed on Easter Sunday to the glorified body. We shall receive the same kind of body but not the same way. Our old bodies where sin dwelt will decay after we leave them behind and the faithful will receive the new glorified body. The Greek word *metaschematidzo* describes this.

Paul affirms this in 1 Corinthians 15:35–44. He likens the spiritual body or resurrection body that emerges from the physical body at death to a plant that emerges from a seed sown in the ground. Our physical bodies are like the outer husk, that part of the seed that dies in the ground, while the glorified body is like the plant that emerges.

Think about It

The bodies of some Christians have been blown up in explosions, burnt with fire, and eaten by animals. The molecules and atoms of those physical bodies are found in the earth, rivers, and seas. God does not have to gather the remains of our physical bodies to transform them. He simply takes His people out of the old body, leaving it behind to decay, and gives them a new body as He takes them home to heaven.

In other words, when the faithful were taken from the earth at Jesus' Return, bodies did not go flying into the air. It would have appeared to others that they simply died. We can see how this event would have gone primarily unnoticed. A large number of bodies would have been found at Pella where the Christians at Jerusalem had fled when it was clear that the beloved city's last days were nearing. That was no unusual event at that time as the Jews and Gentiles were killing each other leaving some cities uninhabited during those tribulation days with its "wars and rumors of wars." Pella was, in fact, one such city vacated after the Jews had killed the Gentile residents in retaliation for their attacks. This became the temporary refuge for the Christians from Jerusalem before they exited earth.

Jesus' Return Back Then Sheds Light on Some Problematic Scriptures

When you see that Jesus returned at the conclusion of the apostolic generation, you can begin to understand some problematic matters in Scripture such as Paul's condoning of slavery and the great limitations on female leadership. Societal reform does not seem to have been on the agenda of the first generation of Christians in a world where Satan was still the ruler. This world would also undergo great upheaval during Jesus' imminent Return. There would be a radical change of management from Satan to Jesus, the faithful would be removed from the earth, and God's wrath would be poured out. The apostles focused on preaching the gospel, making disciples, and building up the Body of Christ in order that converts might mature in preparation for Jesus' Return. They focused on seeing that their lives were changing rather than changing a world that had been under Satan's authority.

This period of great tribulation, I believe, is why the Spirit permitted Paul at that time to accept the institution of slavery, encouraging slaves to be the best workers they could be in those circumstances and masters to treat their slaves properly as they were all being changed. While he clearly led the way in opening the doors for women to assume positions of leadership in the church, first generation Christianity still reflected the male domination that defined life on this earth from the beginning on through the days of the Old Covenant. I believe God knew that societal reform at that time would have been futile in a world that was about to pass through days the likes of which there would never be again according to Jesus. That was difficult enough without adding any further "fuel to the fire."

Things changed in the years following Jesus' Return when He began His reign. Now, nearly two thousand years later, there is clearly a new stance for the Body of Christ. Societal reform is certainly part of the agenda of the new ruler for His people, but He also recognizes the need to transform human lives in order for this to work and the church must lead the way. His strategy is to change the people of this world, gaining their cooperation through the New Covenant as they work with the new ruler who reigns to "make all things new." Since then, the Spirit has clearly revealed God's displeasure with the institution of slavery and His working toward its abolition. He has also elevated woman in the Body of Christ to a new position not enjoyed prior to and during the apostolic generation

Think about It

Paul's position on slavery and women during the first generation of Christianity did not mean the Scriptures were in error as some have said. It simply reflected God's wisdom knowing that radical changes were being made on how to relate to Him moving from the Old Covenant to the New Covenant, from the Jews alone to Jews and Gentiles together, along with all the tribulation related to those last days. Since then, in a world where Jesus now reigns to make all things new in contrast to Satan the destroyer, God's displeasure with the institution of slavery and the inferior treatment of women has become clear. Working with societal issues, building the Body of Christ, and changing lives into the likeness of Christ is the way God works with us to finally bring peace to our world someday.

Why Does John's Gospel Differ from the Others?

Scholars have observed and tried for years to explain why Matthew, Mark, and Luke are very similar, called the synoptic Gospels, while John's Gospel is quite different. John begins his Gospel not at Bethlehem, as do Matthew and Luke, but at the very beginning of time with the assertion that Jesus was the word and all things were created through Him. John wants us to know that Jesus was God, second member of the Godhead. What happened at Bethlehem is summed up in the words: "The word became flesh and dwelt among us" (1:17). John never says anything about the prophecies in the apocalyptic portions of the synoptic Gospels regarding Jesus' Return. He talks about how some are passing from death into life and that those who live and believe in Him will never die.

Years ago, C.H. Dodd, a New Testament scholar, wrote a book about John's Gospel entitled *Realized Eschatology*. While he never came to the conclusions described here, it is interesting to note his overall observation that John's Gospel is written from the perspective that the "last things" have already been realized.

Think about It

When John received the Revelation, which I believe occurred in A.D. 63, the angel told him "You must prophecy again about many peoples, nations, tongues, and kings" (Rev. 10:11). So while the other apostles and New Testament writers would shortly be martyred through Nero's persecution that began in A.D. 64 or taken from the earth at Jesus' Return in A.D. 68, God revealed to John that His work is to continue on earth after that climactic event. Historical records confirm that John lived beyond the end of the first century, A.D. Because John lived through those last days as part of God's plan, he was better able to process the prophecies and the Revelation and understand the significance of what happened during those climactic days. This would explain why John omits the prophecies in his Gospel but talks about truths that depend upon Jesus' Return back then.

One Final Note

Turning the World Right Side Up does not go into detail regarding what those first Christians experienced during the days when Jesus returned. The earlier book, *Bringing Heaven to Earth Because He Has Returned*, provides such information with eighty-one footnotes documenting historical sources back then along with eleven illustrations and tables.

After presenting scriptural and historical data supporting the belief that Jesus returned at the end of the apostolic generation, it then tracks Paul's ministry from his earliest letters to the latest with special attention to what Paul taught about the Return of Christ. It examines important Greek words related to the faith and experience that Paul taught. One such word is *epiphaneia* meaning "the appearing." Only Paul uses this word in the New

Testament, all six times in conjunction with the Return of Jesus. The first three uses in his earlier letters see His Return as yet future. The last three in a later letter view it as an event in the process of happening.

The study of Biblical prophecy becomes much easier when you believe Jesus returned for His first followers. Then, you no longer try to speculate about what current events may be related to the prophecies. Now, you look back after the fact to discover the historical events that fulfilled the prophecies. That is much easier and an exciting study as this author has discovered through the years. *Bringing Heaven to Earth Because He Has Returned* provides much of his research over the past years.

The book also presents a chronological framework for Daniel's Seventieth Week when the second-coming events happened. This will be aided by input from Paul's epistles, the two apocalypses of Daniel and Revelation, and an understanding of the events associated with the third Jewish Festival season consisting of the Feast of Trumpets, the Day of Atonement, and the Feast of Booths. This all comes together in the chapter "Daniel's Seventieth Week as It Happened" (A.D. 63–70) coordinating biblical prophecy, historical events, and the letters of Paul.

The last part of the book deals with the New Testament pathway to the yet unrealized prophetic vision of peace upon the earth. Accomplishing this grand dream does not require any future intervention by God, such as a Second Coming. God is requiring, however, that we learn the obedience God has revealed in Scripture. He needs such cooperation from us to work with His appointed King who reigns over all things, working to make all things new. Disciples, servants, and witnesses in submission to His authority will lead the way to God's grand vision of peace on this earth. *Then, one can only imagine what lies beyond that!*